Services *for the* urban poor

Services *for the* urban poor

2.

Working with Partners

Andrew Cotton & Kevin Tayler

Water, Engineering and Development Centre
Loughborough University
2000

Water, Engineering and Development Centre,
Loughborough University,
Leicestershire, LE11 3TU, UK

© A.P. Cotton and W.K. Tayler, 2000

ISBN 13 Paperback: 978 0 90605 579 3
ISBN Ebook: 9781788533447
Book DOI: http://dx.doi.org/10.3362/9781788533447

A catalogue record for this book is available from the British Library.

A reference copy of this publication is also available online at:
http://www.lboro.ac.uk/wedc/publications/sftup.htm

Cotton, A.P. and Tayler, W.K. (2000)
Services for the Urban Poor:
Section 2. Working with Partners
WEDC, Loughborough University, UK.

WEDC (The Water, Engineering and Development Centre) at Loughborough University in the UK is one of the world's leading institutions concerned with education, training, research and consultancy for the planning, provision and management of physical infrastructure for development in low- and middleincome countries.

This edition is reprinted and distributed by Practical Action Publishing.
Since 1974, Practical Action Publishing has published and disseminated books and information in support of international development work throughout the world. Practical Action Publishing trades only in support of its parent charity objectives and any profits are covenanted back to Practical Action (Charity Reg. No. 247257, Group VAT Registration No. 880 9924 76).

All reasonable precautions have been taken by the WEDC, Loughborough University to verify the information contained in this publication. However, WEDC, Loughborough University does not necessarily endorse the technologies presented in this document. The published material is being distributed without warranty of any kind, either expressed or implied. The responsibility for the interpretation and use of the material lies with the reader. In no event shall the WEDC, Loughborough University be liable for damages as a result of their use.

This document is an output from project R7292 funded by the UK Department for International Development (DFID) for the benefit of low-income countries. The views expressed are not necessarily those of DFID.

Acknowledgements

The financial support of the Department for International Development of the British Government is gratefully acknowledged. The authors would particularly like to thank their many urban engineering colleagues and friends throughout India, Pakistan and Sri Lanka with whom they have worked for the last fifteen years. Their experience has been central to the preparation of this work. Mr P Srinivasa Rao from Hyderabad, India provided a critical review of earlier drafts and additional material for Sections 4 and 6. Colleagues at WEDC and GHK Research and Training provided information and comments throughout the development of the work. We also acknowledge the inclusion of some material from earlier work jointly authored with Dr Richard Franceys. Finally, we wish to acknowledge Sue Cotton for her editorial contributions and the patience and skill of Rod Shaw and Glenda McMahon of the WEDC Publications Office in the design and production of the manual.

Contents

Section 2

Working with Partners

Who should read this
Staff of donor and lending agencies who propose to identify programmes for improving services for the poor in towns and cities; it is also of interest to their partners in national and state level government ministries and departments.

Objectives of this section
To review possible partnering arrangements, the strengths and weaknesses of different institutional options for local programme management and the institutional constraints to the development of an action planning approach to improve services for the urban poor.

What this section tells you
Genuine **partnerships** between NGOs, government institutions and user groups involve long term commitments, equal status in decision making and an element of shared risk.

Involving **locally elected councillors** from the outset of the planning process is an essential part of understanding what is already happening.

User groups are central to understanding the needs and priorities of service users. It is particularly important to take account of existing organisations within communities.

NGOs have an important role to play as intermediaries; they may have a good understanding of local communities and skills in facilitating participatory processes.

External support agencies can be an important catalyst for developing a demand responsive approach in addition to bringing programme finance and technical expertise.

Municipalities are a key institutional partner, having experience in servicing poor areas and wide responsibilities for O&M. They lack organisational autonomy and may have limited capacity.

Urban Development Authorities are more autonomous but have no experience of O&M, rarely use participatory approaches and are unused to dealing with the poor.

Project Cells at the State/National level have a high level of autonomy but are remote from local institutions.

Local **Project Management Units** are popular with external donors because of their autonomy and ability to co-opt a multi-disciplinary team of staff. Nevertheless they have no remit for O&M and there is less chance of mainstreaming innovative approaches.

Full integration of externally funded programmes into the existing structure of municipal government represents an optimum approach for sustaining and replicating action planning approaches.

Key characteristics and **capacity building** requirements for partner institutions include: organisational autonomy; leadership; effective management and administration; commercial, user and O&M orientation; technical capability; human resources development.

Institutional constraints to action planning are serious and include: lack of incentives to change existing planning approach; lack of capacity; low cost recovery for services; lack of internal coordination between municipal departments.

Possibilities for **overcoming constraints** include: identifying cases of good local practice; supporting sound initiatives; capacity building; working with and improving what already exists; identifying incentives; engaging with the local political processes.

Partnership roles and responsibilities

Basic requirements

Developing and implementing Action Plans for improving services for the urban poor involves the development of close relationships between some of the stakeholders:

- individual users and groups of users;
- institutions of local government;
- civil society organisations such as NGOs;
- local political structures; and
- external donor agencies.

Participation has long been used to describe the close involvement of users with the planning, implementation and management of their services. More recently, it has been realised that these relationships can become more complex. Governments and agencies request increased levels of commitment and resources from the users, who respond by making more demands on the project. 'Partnership' is now frequently used to describe these relationships; however, if it is to be taken seriously, the concept of partnership has important implications. Partnership implies:

- relationships between the partners which will extend over a longer period of time than for specific projects and which are more open-ended;

- equal status of the partners in decision making, and dealing with one another on an equal footing when carrying out business; and

- an element of risk-taking; partners have to be willing to share risks in order to reap longer term mutual benefits.

It is important to be clear about this. Where there is no sharing of risk and the parties do not deal on an equal basis, the relationship is closer to that between a contractor and sub-contractor than between partners, and needs to be recognised as such. Different partners have different objectives and it becomes a question of how these can be best aligned. The difficult task of developing partnerships is part of the consensus building component of action planning.

Local politicians as partners

In developing the action planning approach, it is important to engage actively with the local political structures for the following reasons.

- Working with local politicians is an essential part of *understanding what is already happening* and how things work in the town or city; this is central to the action planning approach and has to be done from the outset.

- The Councillor is the key person at the Ward level. S/he often has an allocation of funds to carry out local works, and decides which works will be taken up, both capital and O&M. Nevertheless, the works may be carried out in an uncoordinated ad hoc fashion. Action planning needs to take account of these works, and provides the opportunity to co-ordinate any external programme funding with locally raised resources.

- In some towns and many cities, a large number of relatively junior municipal employees, who carry out key O&M activities for the municipality, work out of the Ward office supervised by the Councillor. These can include: engineering staff of the municipality and of certain line agencies; local tax collectors; junior health officers; sanitary Inspectors; manual labourers including solid waste and drain cleaning workers.

- In some situations, the Mayor has a particularly important role in relation to sanctioning Councillor-based budgets for local improvements. The Mayor can exercise some authority if money needs to be brought back to the municipal centre in order to deal with 'lumpy' investments which benefit the city as a whole.

- The Mayor has an overview of the city; a capable Mayor can help to bring different strands of Action Plans together.

Councillors are the legally elected representatives of the citizens and cannot be overlooked because the external view is that they are 'problematic' and 'unrepresentative' even though the poor have been neglected in many cases. Working with local politicians is difficult; they are important allies, and equally may be in a position to frustrate action planning programmes if they are excluded from the process.

User groups and 'communities' as partners

Improvements to urban services involve collective concerns as well as issues which can be dealt with at the individual or household level. Examples include drainage, paving and solid waste collection which have an important impact on the overall quality of the local living environment. However, the term 'community' can be problematic in the urban context as this implies that there exists a single entity or 'community' which is somehow representative of a collective view. This is rarely the case; there can be divisions related to caste, ethnicity and political allegiance.

User groups and communities can be involved to different extents with the planning of service improvements; the spectrum ranges from being passive receivers of information through to full mobilisation where groups take initiatives themselves. It is very difficult for user groups and communities to go the full way to entering into real partnerships with the formal institutions of government because of the need to genuinely share decision making responsibility. Even where there is strong policy and administrative backing for this, successful cases are often built around specific personal relationships with individual officials.

It is particularly important to take account of existing organisations, groups and power structures within communities and to work through them. Attempts to speed up the process of community participation by trying to by-pass these structures often results in failure; they can be undermined and rendered ineffective by local power brokers. Nevertheless, programmes may decide to set up new organisations in order to target marginalised groups of the poor, or women.

See Section 3a on Preparing Local Action Plans and the associated Tools.

See DFID *Guidance Manual on Water Supply and Sanitation Programmes,* (WELL 1998) section 2.2, page 41 for further details; the above comments are a summary of some of the main issues raised.

NGOs as partners

Civil society organisations including NGOs play a very wide variety of roles including:

- acting as intermediaries in negotiations between service users and government institutions;

- delivering services, including construction of infrastructure;

- advocacy of policy reform: for example, to give greater recognition to the needs of marginalised groups; and

- promotion of single issue agendas, for example specific improvements to the environment.

NGOs range in size, complexity and outreach from international and national level organisations through to small local groups. They provide a very important intermediary function in a wide variety of situations including: channelling resources through to community-based organisations and user groups; capacity building to support the development of local participation in decision making and dealing with government; and providing technical assistance.

NGOs have certain advantages as intermediaries:

- a good understanding of local communities, their needs and priorities;

- familiarity with local innovations and sometimes with appropriate technological solutions; and

- flexibility to adapt to the needs of the moment; this can be valuable where they can adapt their skills in facilitating participatory processes to the particular requirements of local action planning for urban services improvement programmes.

See Tool 3 for information on the role of NGOs as intermediaries.

See DFID *Guidance Manual on Water Supply and Sanitation Programmes,* (WELL 1998) section 2.2, page 50 for further details; the above comments are a summary of some of the main issues raised.

External donor agencies as partners

External agencies have an important potential role in acting as a catalyst for developing action planning approaches which are much more demand responsive than might currently be the case. External agencies often bring finance, technical expertise and other international experience as part of their package, and as such are accorded a high status by government institutions and officials. It is therefore important that the basic tenets of partnership are not forgotten, and that the agencies do not try to exert excessive leverage.

One of their key roles is to provide support and capacity building for the local institution which is ultimately responsible for developing and implementing Action Plans. Developing new processes such as action planning within local institutions is a long term activity which can be very time consuming and require a lot of management inputs. There has to be a commitment to invest quite heavily in this support and capacity building without expecting to see immediate concrete results and outputs on the ground.

A probable long term objective of an external agency is that the process of action planning developed in one or more towns and cities is replicated on a state-wide or nation-wide basis. In this, the relationship between the external agency and state or national government is crucial. It is at this higher level that there exists the potential for institutionalising new planning processes into the procedures which will be followed at lower levels of government, for example at the municipal level.

Local institutions as partners
This is a central to the whole issue of partnerships and is dealt with in detail in the following parts of this section of the manual.

Which local institution?
Programmes for improving urban services are delivered through local institutions; the 'institutional home' influences planning, implementation and the subsequent sustainability of the project with regard to effective operation and maintenance. It is important that donor agencies and their partners in government take post-project sustainability into account at this stage. There is a natural tendency to focus on those institutional arrangements which lead to ease of planning and implementation, which are not necessarily those which will have ultimate responsibility for O&M.

The characteristics of the relevant secondary stakeholders were outlined in Section 1; Table 2.1 describes the key features, advantages and disadvantages of different institutional partners.

Table 2.1. Potential institutional arrangements

Municipalities	**Key features**
	Municipalities are a key institutional partner because they have statutory responsibility for a wide range of service provision. Even where construction has been vested with a different agency, they are often still responsible for O&M. In the past, there has been a reluctance to engage with municipalities partly because of actual and/or perceived political interference in programme management. Local Councillors are the political representatives at the Municipal level.
	Advantages
	■ Wide responsibilities for O&M of services
	■ Potential accountability to users
	■ Experienced in dealing with citizens and their political representatives
	■ Experienced in service improvements in urban poor areas
	■ Opportunity to integrate the programme with existing initiatives
	Disadvantages
	■ Lack of organisational autonomy for effective management
	■ Lack of co-ordination between departments responsible for the different urban services
	■ Inadequate systems for financial planning and management
	■ Lack of professional capacity to take on complex programmes
	■ Unpredictable financial position which depends upon transfer payments from higher tiers of government

Table 2.1. continued

Specialist agencies	**Key features** Urban Development Authorities (UDAs) exist in many large urban centres and often have semi-autonomous status. They are usually charged with developing long term plans for urban development, and with developing sites for commercial and residential use. They have frequently been selected as the key partner for implementing urban service improvement programmes. Other line agencies with responsibilities for water supply and power supply are less appropriate as main partners due to their specific sector focus. **Advantages** ■ Some professional capacity in planning is available, with experience of developing city-wide plans ■ Lack of political dimension makes it simpler for donors, particularly regarding implementation of physical works ■ Semi-autonomous status gives greater independence in management **Disadvantages** ■ No remit to deal with O&M; new facilities require different institutional arrangements for O&M ■ Available skills largely limited to traditional physical masterplanning ■ Predominantly staffed by planners and engineers with no experience of participatory approaches to planning ■ Lack of direct local accountability; unused to dealing with citizens ■ Little experience of dealing with improvements in urban poor areas

Table 2.1. continued	
Project cells at the State/National level	**Key features** In cases where no local institution has been identified as being appropriate, a 'cell' is created within a state or national level ministry with responsibility for a specific externally funded programme in a town or city. This has some characteristics of a Project Management Unit (PMU), which is considered below in more detail. **Advantages** ■ High level of autonomy, with selected staff appointed to the cell ■ Funding agency can exercise close control over finance and implementation **Disadvantages** ■ Remote from other local institutions with little opportunity for lessons to be learned and absorbed locally ■ Little experience of local conditions and institutional issues ■ Lack of local accountability ■ No remit to deal with O&M

Table 2.1. continued	
Project Management Unit (PMU)	**Key features** A common mechanism for implementing externally funded programmes is to create a dedicated PMU within the particular institution which is the overall host. This should be local but in some cases may end up closer to a 'cell' within a higher level of government. The PMU is responsible for delivering all of the components of the programme, but may in practice subcontract some primary and secondary works to specialist line agencies. **Advantages** ■ The opportunity to co-opt a multil-disciplinary team of staff: technical, social, financial, administrative, gender, human resource development and health promotion ■ Staff are not diverted to carry out other work for the host institution ■ High level of autonomy enables financial disbursement mechanisms to be more transparent **Disadvantages** ■ Created only for implementation, subsequently disbanded without developing a lasting ownership of the programme ■ Relationships with other departments and delegated authority of PMU staff are often not clear ■ Staff disperse back to their 'parent' organisations and opportunities for integrating the lessons from the programme are lost ■ Less chance of 'mainstreaming' innovative approaches ■ No remit to deal with O&M; there have to be incentives for the PMU to take the planning of O&M seriously ■ Bypassing apparently bureaucratic procedures is an illusory benefit and may be a significant disadvantage in mainstreaming new approaches, which have to be able to operate within, or with the minimum of amendment to, existing procedures

Despite their apparent long term disadvantages, PMUs remain a popular option with both donors and partner governments, as they are administratively neat and transparent. Ideally, for an urban service improvement programme the PMU should reside within the municipality. The key issue is how to ensure that co-ordinating mechanisms with the relevant line departments (engineering, health, community development/poverty alleviation) are put in place, so that duplication and overlap are avoided and inter-departmental learning is promoted. In practice, slowness in seconding staff and in replacing staff can be a problem.

Fully integrated programmes

The optimum solution is *full integration* of an externally funded programme into the existing structure of municipal government. In South Asia, the structure is based around the administrative unit of the Municipal Ward, which are sometimes grouped into 'zones' or 'circles'. Wards are the key units as far as implementation of minor new works and O&M of existing works are concerned. Councillors often have access to an annual budget for making local improvements to urban services through new construction and rehabilitation. These 'Councillor schemes' are traditionally identified as a result of discussions between Councillors as representatives of their constituents needs and the relevant Departments of the Municipality. Important O&M activities which may function from the Ward Office include solid waste collection, drain cleaning, street cleaning, staffing of public latrines.

In this approach of full integration, work is classified into externally funded Programme Works and General Works which are undertaken as part of the annual municipal workplan. Implementation of service improvements of the externally funded programme through the Zonal and Ward structure presents major opportunities to achieve the following:

- better integration of planning between general Municipal and programme funded work;

- mainstreaming of innovative approaches to local planning;

- co-ordination and integration of Local plans and Municipal plans;

- developing the framework for consensus building, which needs to operate at a very local level, such as the Municipal Ward;

- compatibility with and lack of duplication of the Councillor-sponsored schemes;

- clear ownership of the programme by the Municipality at the grass roots level of Zones and Wards;

- use of existing capacity within the zonal offices;

- a clear association of the externally funded programme with locally based structures both administratively and politically; this is likely to be a key factor both for sustaining and replicating the programme approaches; and

- implementation by those having an intimate knowledge of the project areas.

Staff work on both externally funded Programme Works and General Works; additional staff funded by the programme can be distributed on a Zonal basis to cope with increased workloads as and when necessary. This is in keeping with the way that municipal line departments function; it therefore avoids a number of detailed but crucial administrative problems relating to staff status and delegated authority, which inevitably arise when new administrative structures are set up for externally funded programmes. There is a need to ensure accountability and transparency in the externally funded programme which satisfies both the Municipality and the external donor. Local Programme Sector Managers can be delegated to operate functionally on the externally funded programme, so that all the information related to the programme flows through them. This is crucial both for the requirements of the management information systems and to establish accountability in the disbursement of programme funds. Below this level, programme posts are distributed zonally as described above.

This approach is also particularly appropriate for regional 'small towns' urban service improvement programmes which cover a number of towns or smaller cities. There has to be close integration with the local municipalities as it becomes impractical to devise new institutional arrangements on such a wide scale and the implementation becomes very remote from O&M (see disadvantages of the State/National level cell).

What to look for

Having reviewed the main characteristics of potential local partner institutions, it is useful to draw up a checklist of issues which are relevant to the development of an action planning approach to improve services for the urban poor. These issues should be explored by the donors of externally funded programmes in collaboration with state or national government partners. Note that no known institution will meet all of the proposed criteria; we are looking for the institutional framework with the *potential* to develop and deliver innovative approaches. The checklist is a useful starting point for developing an agenda for local capacity building and for reviewing the need for external programme support in that institution.

This brief checklist is categorised in accordance with section 2.6 of the DFID *Guidance Manual on Water Supply and Sanitation Programmes* (WELL 1998); this should be referred to for more detailed guidance on institutional appraisal and development.

Table 2.2. Checklist of issues for local institutional partners	
Category	**Issues**
Organisational autonomy	■ How easily can both the donor/government and the local institution adapt and develop administrative requirements for action planning ■ Ability to make decisions about hiring staff and developing inter-disciplinary ways of working between internal departments
Leadership	■ Existence of potential Project Champions at a senior level with the potential to influence the direction of a programme
Effective management and administration	■ Experience of management of special government programmes, external donor funded programmes and dealing with donors ■ Existence and extent of strategic plans in any areas, involving forward planning and thinking ahead
Commercial orientation	■ Extent of cost recovery for services provided ■ Experience of managing non-standard financing mechanisms: small project funds; social funds; challenge funds
User orientation	■ Experience of and attitude towards working with user groups in participation and planning ■ Making use of and working together with support groups such as NGOs and external consultants to improve interactions with user groups
O&M orientation	■ Extent of involvement in O&M and likely sustainability of new facilities ■ Existence of strategic plans for O&M ■ Means of raising revenue to finance O&M

Table 2.2. continued	
Category	**Issues**
Technical capability	■ Nature of work and typical workloads; will the programme swamp the institution ■ Ability to handle projects with different infrastructure components which has a strong participatory approach ■ Experience of delivering services to the urban poor ■ Skills mix of staff: availability of different disciplinary skills at senior, middle and junior levels ■ Experience of managing software such as participatory planning and promotion activities e.g. in health and education ■ Experience of undertaking similar work in the past
Human resources development	■ Have the training needs of any staff been analysed or dealt with
Organisational culture	■ Evidence of willingness to adopt new approaches to dealing with the problems of the poor ■ Experience of working with external consultants, donor, NGOs, other support agents
Interactions with external institutions	■ Links to higher level (state/national) institutions, likelihood of models & processes being adopted and institutionalised ■ Links with other service providing institutions at the local level

Practical problems with action planning

It is important to be realistic about the problems of developing action planning approaches which respond to the demands of the urban poor. The constraints are severe, and there will be situations where the approach is not workable. Table 2.3 describes some typical constraints which can be encountered in the South Asian context. At the outset, it is important to realise that the baseline capacity for embarking on a complex process at the municipal level may be very low.

Table 2.3. Potential constraints to the adoption of action planning approaches

Constraint	Comment
Existing planning procedures	■ There is no culture of municipal planning in the sense understood by international agencies. Municipalities essentially follow rules and procedures laid down by the state or centre for implementing programmes. ■ Broad-brush strategic planning is not commonly undertaken; feasibility stages are rarely seen and the norm is to opt for the construction of new facilities in accordance with standards and norms rather than on responding to user demand and improving O&M of existing infrastructure. ■ There is no incentive to develop a problem solving approach grounded in 'situation analysis' which is the first step in any logical planning process.
Local institutions	■ Responsibilities for different services are split between different institutions (e.g.water, power, drainage); there is little incentive for co-operation within existing structures. ■ Within one institution there may be little co-ordination between different departments delivering services which complement one another. ■ It is difficult to identify a lead department to take on innovative action planning. ■ Links with NGOs and the informal sector are poorly developed and often not accepted as part of working practice.
Incentives for change	■ What are the incentives for each stakeholder to change the way they currently operate? Why should local government adopt new approaches such as action planning which are demand-based? This is the heart of the problem; an understanding of this is essential in order to unlock many of the problems. ■ Municipalities generally have limited vision and hence limited capacity to either change themselves or provide leadership in the development and implementation of new ideas and approaches. While 'pathfinder' organisations do at times develop ideas at the local level, these ideas cannot be translated into general practice without structures that are designed to allow this to happen.

Table 2.3. continued	
Constraint	**Comment**
	■ Pressure for change at the municipal level must normally come from above or below, in other words from higher levels of government or the community - perhaps through their elected representatives. The most effective pressure for change may occur when the two are combined.
Lack of capacity	■ The lack of basic technical and managerial skills at the municipal level is a fundamental constraint. This tends to foster a culture of ad-hoc approaches that pay little attention to longer-term needs relating to planning and maintenance. ■ It is in general unrealistic to expect municipal staff to think through complex issues and develop innovative practices. ■ There is a need for realism in what can be delivered locally when dealing with complex issues and new concepts such as demand. Buzzwords on the international agenda have very little place in the lexicon of municipal government.
Cost recovery	■ Financing and cost recovery have to be considered as part of the total picture of municipal finance and not just as issues related to programmes for improving services to the urban poor. ■ This may only make sense in the wider context of reform of municipal finance. ■ In South Asia there are significant practical problems recovering the recurrent costs for municipal services. The main mechanism is through charges which are related to property tax; municipalities either find it difficult or have little incentive to raise the level of tax collection.

A critical part of implementing any action planning process involves addressing typical constraints such as these; there are simply no easy answers. Some suggested approaches are given in Table 2.4; these depend to a large extent on the willingness of all parties to invest time and effort in developing a partnership approach as discussed previously.

Table 2.4. Overcoming constraints

Approach	Comment
Good local practice	■ Look for local actions which provide the opportunity for real innovation. Key areas are the generation of demand in low income areas through local planning with the help of intermediaries. ■ Pilot activities provide a useful opportunity for this.
Support good initiatives	■ Identify and support town or city institutions which are good performers. Learn from them, institutionalise and apply procedures via the State or National government who have a central role to play in developing and applying innovative practices such as action planning. ■ These practices need to be perceived by local implementing agencies as being part of State/National procedures.
Capacity building	■ One of the most important issues, and a key role for the external donor agency.
Working with what is there	■ Work on new initiatives needs to be complemented by working within existing government programmes which are tackling services for the urban poor. Whilst these are rarely popular with donors, particularly if traditional approaches to subsidy are involved, such programmes are unlikely to go away. It is better to accept the fact and work towards marginal improvement in their operations by working on change from within. ■ This can be a vehicle for improving capacity to manage the programmes more effectively.
Taking action	■ It is important to take some demonstrative action to show commitment and a serious purpose; years of studies and what are often perceived locally as "hot air" discussions can have negative effects. This is not advocating endless ad hoc interventions; these demonstrative actions do need to be incorporated into the overall strategy. Pilot work needs to develop a critical mass and be backed up with sufficient funding. ■ At the same time it is difficult to maintain a realistic balance between what needs to be known for long-term planning and what is needed for short term interventions.

Table 2.4. continued

Approach	Comment
Incentives	■ It is essential that local politicians buy in to any incentive-based approach, whether at the state-to-municipal level, or the municipal-to-neighbourhood/household level. ■ A wider civil society issue is the apparent lack of public pressure for better services. This could come by demonstration by example: e.g. where there are good levels of service such as 24 hour water supply.
Engage with the local political processes	■ Local political processes are crucial. Whilst (ideally) the State promotes good practice which is enshrined in its procedures and instructions to municipal government, it may still require the Mayor to pull together the various strands at the local level.

Now read on

Section 3 of the Manual goes into the detail of developing Action Plans. This is relevant for:

■ local Programme Directors, Programme Sector Managers and their staff who are responsible for developing and implementing Action Plans for improving services for the poor in towns and cities;
■ also Programme Sector Managers from the donor agencies and technical support partners including NGOs and local/international consultants.

References

WELL, (1998) *Guidance Manual on Water Supply and Sanitation Programmes.*